Copyright © 2022 Sobia Publication

All rights reserved

The characters and events portrayed in this book are fictitious. Any similarity to real persons, living or dead, is coincidental and not intended by the author.

No part of this book may be reproduced, or stored in a retrieval system, or transmitted in any form or by any means, electronic, mechanical, photocopying, recording, or otherwise, without express written permission of the publisher.

Cover design by: Art Painter
Library of Congress Control Number: 2018675309
Printed in the United States of America

CW01284198

CUSTOMER SERVICE, CUSTOMER SUPPORT, AND CUSTOMER EXPERIENCE

Customer Service, Customer Support, and Customer Experience Training. Loyal Clients Through World-Class Customer Service

Sobia Publication

CONTENTS

Title Page
Copyright
What you'll learn — 1
About The Book — 2
Who this book is for — 5
Chapter 1: Introduction — 6
Chapter 2: Diagnostic Intro — 8
Chapter 3: Conflict Types — 10
Chapter 4: Conflict Types in CM — 14
Chapter 5: Rule Analysis and Adaptation — 15
Chapter 6: Rule Analysis and Adaptation in CM — 20
Chapter 7: Techniques Introduction — 21
Chapter 8: Respect and Understanding — 23
Chapter 9: Respect and Understanding in CM — 29
Chapter 10: Comforting and Supporting — 31
Chapter 11: Comforting and Supporting in CM — 36
Chapter 12: Mediation and Diplomacy — 37
Chapter 13: Mediation and Diplomacy in CM — 41
Chapter 14: Personal Rules/Boundaries — 43
Chapter 15: Personal Rules/Boundaries in CM — 48
Chapter 16: Implementation Focus — 50

Chapter 17: Implementation Focus in CM	55
Chapter 18: Traps Introduction	56
Chapter 19: Misalignment Traps	58
Chapter 20: Misalignment Traps in CM	63
Chapter 21: Escalation Traps	65
Chapter 22: Escalation Traps in CM	69
Chapter 23: Conclusion	70
About The Author	73
Books By This Author	75

WHAT YOU'LL LEARN

- Customer service to build super-fans who buy more and recommend your business to their friends
- Create a customer experience that delights clients and makes them feel like they are getting a great product
- Make more money from repeat customers and referrals
- Turn even angry clients into loyal, long-term clients through amazing customer service
- Engage your customers in a better way
- Make customers love you
- You'll learn how to properly analyze clients' rules and how to avoid breaking them, avoiding future conflicts
- You'll learn how to mediate tense situations between clients and the organisation, evaluating both positions impartially
- You'll learn how to avoid the common traps in terms of conflicts, which can actually make a conflict worse

ABOUT THE BOOK

Customer experience is when you proactively provide great customer care, delight people, and turn them into raving super-fans.

Customer service is when you reactively deal with customer problems, delight them, and turn them into raving super-fans.

Use customer service and customer experience to create happy customers even if at first you have to deal with upset customers and turn them into superfans.

Use customer service and customer experience as marketing and branding strategies because they help you sell more.

I consider good customer service an advanced strategy for entrepreneurs because new entrepreneurs tend to focus on getting their next client and typically don't delight their current customers. But once you start giving your client outstanding customer experience, they begin to buy from you again and even tell their friends.

So you don't have to chase new customers. Just delight existing clients and they'll be the ones who will talk about your business and bring their friends to you.

Experienced entrepreneurs understand that it isn't enough to just create an OK product. Your product must delight and WOW your customers. And a part of delighting your customers is providing great customer service that inspires positive reactions and emotions in your customers.

Once you inspire positive reactions and emotions in your customers, they will subconsciously feel that your product is better than it actually is. Your customers will also associate your business with their positive emotions.

TURN ANGRY AND UNHAPPY CUSTOMERS INTO LOYAL CLIENTS WITH CUSTOMER SERVICE

Angry customers are not wrong, crazy, or mean. They are just frustrated and they want your product to work for them. If you provide great customer service, respect them, listen to them, and offer a great solution that works and fixes their problems, you can turn them into clients who are loyal long-term.

WHAT IS CUSTOMER EXPERIENCE AND HOW IT IS DIFFERENT FROM CUSTOMER SUPPORT

Customer experience is different from customer service. Customer experience is a proactive approach where you create ways to identify good clients and give them a better customer experience. For example, give them something for free when it's their birthday. They will appreciate that and become more loyal as customers. Customer experience is proactive whereas customer support is reactive.

BOOK MATERIAL IS FROM SUCCESSFUL PERSONAL EXPERIENCE AND INDUSTRY GOOD PRACTICES

Once I started applying the customer experience ideas in this book, it caused more positive responses from my customers, more sales, more repeat customers, more good reviews, and business growth. I rarely see other entrepreneurs apply these strategies, which is why I feel that they are only used by advanced and experienced entrepreneurs. Customer support isn't hard. It just requires care and attentiveness.

SOBIA PUBLICATION

POWERFUL CUSTOMER SERVICE AND CUSTOMER EXPERIENCE SKILLS THAT GIVE YOU AN ADVANTAGE

People often want formulas or practical blueprints for what to do. This book will give you the customer service and customer experience skills that will give you an advantage over your competition by retaining loyal customers who buy more from you long-term.

RESPONSIVE AND CARING INSTRUCTOR: WORLD-CLASS STUDENT SUPPORT

Invest in your future. Get today, improve your customer service, and see your business grow.

WHO THIS BOOK IS FOR

- Entrepreneurs and small business owners who need to do customer support
- You're anybody dealing with customers (high- or low-value, high- or low-touch), and especially dealing with unhappy ones
- You're anybody in Customer Success or Customer Service
- You're anybody in Client Relations or Investor Relations

CHAPTER 1: INTRODUCTION

Hi and welcome to the Customer Service, Customer Support, And Customer Experience book in this book, we are going to cover it, how to resolve conflicts, but not just that. We are going to split this process into several stages from diagnosing the conflict to not falling into basic traps when executing that resolution. Without further ado, let's take a look at our goals and the structure of the book.

Welcome to Customer Service, Customer Support, And Customer Experience. In this chapter, we are going to learn how to properly de-escalate and resolve conflicts and their situations with others to achieve a common goal in terms of goals. Our major goal in this chapter is to effectively address and resolve conflicts. That's what we're here for.

But more specifically in detail, we are going to learn how to assess the different conflict types groups into hot and cold as well. Is this specific breach of rules that causes the conflict in the first place, how to properly calm down and empathize with the other person or mediate conflicts between two third parties?

How do you avoid the common traps that cause an escalation of the situation, such as disrespecting or belittling the other side? How to avoid misalignment traps that will cause other conflicts, such as not aligning expectations or promising things that you can't deliver.

And finally, how to properly support and comfort others when they are emotional, for example. Among other things, to achieve this, we are going to focus on three different dimensions of conflicts, free families of techniques, if you will.

The first is diagnostic, properly assessing what type of conflict you have on your hands, as well as what led up to it in the first place. Then actual techniques to use empathy, focusing on implementation, personal boundaries, and others that help you solve the conflict.

And finally will take a look at, both in terms of mismatches and expectations, but also escalation traps that can make a situation much worse. So, as you see, we are going to explore conflict resolution in three main stages. Without further ado, let's dive into the first one.

CHAPTER 2: DIAGNOSTIC INTRO

Let's talk about diagnosing conflicts before you even try to resolve a conflict. It's important to know the cause of it. Of course, in many cases, there may be an urgency and you need to just get this fixed. But if you don't know what the reason is, it's just going to happen again and again.

So it's important to leverage some tools to know what caused the conflict. And that's exactly what we're going to talk about before handling a conflict. It's crucial to properly analyze what type of conflict it is and what led to it in the first place because although the techniques used to deal with the conflict will be mostly the same, knowing what triggered it and what type of conflict it is important at least to know how to prevent it in the future by addressing the specific trigger to things that are essential to know at this diagnostic stage are both how the people are behaving, the different types of reactions, hot or cold conflicts, and also what rule violations caused the conflict in the first place.

Because every conflict means that somebody has a rule and somebody else violated that rule. To cover this initial diagnostic phase, we are then going to focus on these two key areas. The first is the types of conflicts, the types of reactions that people may have avoiding being aggressive, withdrawing, poisoning, others, being passive-aggressive, and more.

Then we'll take a look at the specific rules that people have that cause a conflict when they are broken in how to adapt to them, to fight them in the future. It's important to know whether these rules may be reasonable or not. For example, a person may have a rule every time that someone raises their voice.

I feel disrespected, which may be reasonable, but another person may have a rule that every time that someone questions me, even if they're right, I feel disrespected, which may not be that easy to justify. So as you see, we are going to analyze both the conflict type and the rules that caused it. Without further ado, let's take a look at them.

CHAPTER 3: CONFLICT TYPES

Let's talk about conflict types, not all conflicts are equal. And people can have a lot of different reactions, but we can usually group conflicts into two major groups, which are hot conflicts and cause conflicts. And although you can use the same tools for both, it's important to understand the differences between both.

Let's take a look. When a conflict does break out, people can have many different reactions. It's funny that when you think of conflict, you probably think of two people arguing loudly over each other in shouting matches. But in reality, conflicts come in many shapes and sizes in all of them.

Make no mistake, it must be considered a conflict. Someone avoiding something being passive-aggressive or others are all forms of conflict. And the way to deal with this is also mostly the same. Nevertheless, it's important to realize the different types of conflict that you may be dealing with.

One possibility is that the person may just outright avoid the issue, pretend that it didn't happen, or pretend to agree just to force compliance. Another possibility is that the person may bottle things up at the cost of becoming more and more stressed and possibly once they can't take it anymore, they eventually blow up in your face.

Another possibility is that the person may become more aggressive, even being verbally abusive, or just taking an accusatory stance. Being defensive or another possibility is that they may become passive-aggressive, sabotaging things on purpose to make their point without a confrontation or even poisoning the people behind the scenes.

Despite the different types of reactions, these can usually be grouped in a very broad sense into hot or cold conflicts. Hot conflicts are the ones based on too much intensity, aggressiveness, insults, and verbal abuse. It's what you probably think of when you think of a conflict called conflict.

The ones are based on a lack of communication. So passive-aggressiveness voluntarily withdrawing, avoiding the topic, even becoming delusional and ignoring the facts or pretending that everything is fine or fits this pattern. While the general way to address both of these is usually the same, we're going to take a look at it, including techniques such as applying empathy, showing respect, and making the person feel understood in trying to reach an equitable conclusion for both sides.

It's important to add an extra layer of understanding in hot conflicts so that you can slowly calm down an aggressive person and bring them back down to the realm of logic so that they're reasonable enough for cold conflicts to proactively stimulate communication because the person is going to withdraw and you need to be the one to slowly bring them out.

What are some implementation pointers in terms of the different conflict types? The first is objectivity. Despite the type of conflict, the remaining objective is always essential if the other side feels these respective ignored or victimized in some way.

Things will get worse, and in many cases, they already do this. Even if you are objective, if you're not, it'll be even worse. The second is that people can have wild swings. People usually do have one pattern. Some just avoid it.

Some just become aggressive and so on. Sure. But people can swing wildly. For example, someone who is very aggressive can be put in their place, and in the future, they don't speak their mind anymore because they're stubborn or they're pouting.

But on the other hand, someone with a conflict that is withdrawn and is blowing things up and doesn't speak up may end up going up and becoming very aggressive when they actually can't take it anymore. Diagnosing is crucial as people can have so many different reactions. It's important to assess the ones they may have when something may be wrong with them.

There may be a conflict there. And finally, remember that all of these types are conflicts. Conflicts are not just when people are aggressive and in each other's faces. All of these types are conflicts and should be taken seriously.

Why are some do's and don'ts of the different conflict types? Do you have that weird, awkward conversation to figure out what may be wrong with someone? It's better to have a small conflict now than let it grow into a bigger one later. Don't assume that both conflicts are not conflicts behind every attitude of withdrawing and avoiding.

There is a reason, and chances are this situation could have been finessed. What are some examples of the different conflict types? The first is a screaming match. Again, it's probably what you think of when you think of a conflict, two people being aggressive, and shouting at each other's faces.

It's not the only type, but it is a type. Another example is someone being passive-aggressive. They don't fight the other person openly, they poison other people behind their back or they sabotage what the person wants to do. Make no mistake, this is a type of conflict as well.

And finally, avoidance is when someone avoids a person or a topic that they just don't want to deal with, that is a conflict. They may be trying to avoid a confrontation, ironically, but avoidance itself is a type of conflict. What are our key takeaways here?

The first is that there are multiple types of conflict. Everyone deals with things in their way. So conflict comes in many shapes and sizes. But all of these conflicts must be handled, usually in the same way. Then the different types of conflicts can be broadly grouped into hot and cold ones.

While hot conflicts are about aggressiveness and intensity, caused conflicts are about avoidance and we've drawn in. Remember that you can find all key takeaways on the key takeaways wiki page. Both the link and the passwords are in the book description for convenience so that you can just copy and paste them. So as you see, conflicts can be grouped into hot or cold.

Although the tools that we're going to use are going to be mostly the same for both types, it's important to keep in mind that for hot conflicts, the person is aggressive and they need to calm down, and in conflicts, the person is just withdrawing in. They need to connect with you more.

CHAPTER 4: CONFLICT TYPES IN CM

All the steps that you will take to resolve a customer problem will be mostly the same. It's still important to know whether the conflict is hot or cold in a hot conflict. The client will be aggressive, maybe screaming in your face, pointing out how you and your company are incompetent, making threats, and so on.

In a cold one, they will probably withdraw, not speak to you, share less with you, not trust you as much, and simply disappear after some time and stop being a client. Both kids need attention for hot conflicts. Focus more on empathizing until the person calms down while four cool conflicts focus more on actively drawing out their objections. But ultimately, the techniques that we will use to solve conflicts will work for both. It's just important to know this.

CHAPTER 5: RULE ANALYSIS AND ADAPTATION

Let's talk about rules because as personal development expert Tony Robbins would say, every upset is a rule that is upset. Usually, conflicts are not random. They occur because you disrespect someone or you speak over them or you cut them off or you trigger a very specific break, any very specific rule.

And this is useful because if you can find out which rule you broke, you can avoid breaking it again. Let's take a look. As we mentioned, all conflicts come from a person triggering another one by breaking one of their rules. And these can be very generic or very specific, very explicit, depending on the person enforcement pairs of people.

These can be in direct conflict. Let me give you some examples. I may have an implicit rule of if you interrupt me when I'm speaking, I will feel disrespected. On the other hand, you may have a rule that it's OK to interrupt everybody else and they can interrupt me as well.

You can see how these two rules can create a conflict between these two people, especially if each side is not aware that the other side has an opposing rule. This can degenerate very quickly. Or I may have an implicit rule of if you market yourself and you publicize yourself with no results, you're not authentic. While the other side may have a rule.

It's important to draw attention to yourself above all others at all costs. And then you can see how these two people can very easily. And again, it'll be even worse if they're not aware of each other's rules. So whenever a conflict occurs, it's important to diagnose what rules each side has for being disrespected so that you can identify which one was broken for each side, possibly only one side.

This allows each side to respect the other side's rules once they are clarified, and apologize for having broken them. If that's the case, find a compromise in the future. Now, here's the thing. In some cases, the rule is obvious. You can ask somebody why their colleague disrespected them, and they'll say openly while he called me an idiot.

The case is pretty clear cut, and you know who needs to change their behavior to avoid these conflicts in the future? But in some cases, it's going to be more subtle. It can be because someone is something or someone did something that would not always be wrong. But in specific circumstances, for example, someone taking a lead in a project without explicitly having been assigned that either.

And without having validated this with either people in the group or, for example, someone taking the weave when there is a superior present that is being overtaken in a way. In this case, the solution is always to ask questions to find out. Ask people what, in specific, made them feel angry or upset or broke the rules. And so we uncover what the original trigger was, as well as the person's behavior leading up to it.

What are some implementation pointers in terms of uncovering and adapting to people's rules when first realizing that com-

CUSTOMER SERVICE, CUSTOMER SUPPORT, AND CUSTOMER EXPERIENCE

promise is necessary in many cases? There are situations where the rules are simply incompatible. For example, if you have an introvert that always speaks when others are done speaking, an extrovert will keep on speaking and hammering until they are interrupted.

In those cases, both people need to change. Remember that as with many things in life, this is a process, and covering a rule and getting a commitment from someone that they will adapt is not going to magically fix things. It's the beginning of a process, and there can be some subsequent bumps in the road. Until you're in the clear.

A fourth point is to take into account the company culture. Does a specific rule go against the company culture? For example, being an introvert is perfectly fine. But if you are in a department where people solve crises, you must intervene quickly and take action. If someone does not voice their opinion quickly and waits too long. That rule can go against the expected behaviors and culture of the company or their team, at least. And finally, remember that people-I take what they say with a grain of salt.

In some cases, people just snap, and there was no particular rule broken. In some cases, someone felt offended, but the other side didn't offend them or someone was provoked. But the other side conveniently forgets to mention the provocation. Don't be too quick to force specific people to take specific behaviors until it's clear why this conflict occurred.

What are some do's and don'ts in terms of analyzing and adapting to rules? Do try to clarify as much as possible. If the rule isn't clear, you don't have a rule. I just felt offended. Is worthless. I feel offended when someone calls me incompetent is much better. Don't consider rules absolute. When the rule is ridiculous, by all means, request to change the rules. I feel that if people don't support my opinion and don't choose it in every case, it is not just unreasonable. They are plain crazy.

In these cases, you have to politely tell the person that they are the ones who must change. What are some examples of rules? The first is people that have a rule of others not raising their voices. I can have a rule dictating that if you raise your voice. This conversation is over, and I may even decide to leave.

This can be a completely reasonable rule. Someone may have a rule of others not questioning them. Under any circumstance, if anyone dares to challenge what they have to say, even in a polite manner, the person will become defensive or aggressive. This one is not that reasonable and not that easy to justify. And finally, someone we have a rule of others not going behind your back.

They want to act as the gatekeeper for all information and not allow other people to speak among themselves. This can either be a legitimate organizational structure demand, or it can just be the person being controlled due to their insecurity. And in that case, this rule is also hard to justify.

Finally, what are our key takeaways here? The first is that everyone has rules in every conflict caused by a breach of one of those rules. The person may have that rule explicitly or subconsciously, but the violation is the same regardless of the case. The second is that it's crucial to clarify rules regardless of whether the person explicitly knows the rule or not.

They must communicate with the other person. Otherwise, they can't avoid the other person breaking it again in the future. Rules can be reasonable or not. Some may be completely understandable, such as refusing to continue an argument when someone becomes emotional or aggressive, but others can be unfair and not tolerated. And finally, the goal of analyzing someone's rules is always to find a way to not break them later on to avoid subsequent conflicts.

And remember that you can find all key takeaways on the key takeaways wiki page. Both the Wink and the password are in the book description for convenience so that you can just copy and paste them so easily. See NBC, although the biggest priority may be to resolve the conflict right away whenever you can. It's important to talk to the other person and figure out which was the specific rule that caused this conflict so that you can avoid breaking it in the future.

CHAPTER 6: RULE ANALYSIS AND ADAPTATION IN CM

With clients, the rules broken are usually very simple, and they are not so much personal as corporate. It's that, for example, the specific product or service was supposed to work, but it just didn't in some way. So naturally, this already tells you how to avoid future conflicts, and avoid having that product disappoint the person in the future.

But there may also be other reasons here. For example, rolling out a pricing change that makes things more expensive without having informed the customer first or even having already informed them, not having actively communicated in the first twenty-four hours or even less when an emergency occurs, making it seem like you just don't care.

Ignoring an important person in the client company and speaking with another one, for example, when your point of contact is not available and something is urgent and you go above it for each one of these, solving the problem is naturally always the priority. But after this is taken care of, the next priority should always be to identify what was the trigger for the situation and avoid triggering it in the future.

CHAPTER 7: TECHNIQUES INTRODUCTION

Let's talk about the techniques now that you've properly assessed what caused this conflict and what type of conflict it is, it's not time to use a couple of weapons to resolve the conflict. Let's take a look. If you properly assess the conflict that you have on your hands now, it's time to solve it using a myriad of techniques and tools, the different techniques that will cover or have elements in common, namely showing empathy and understanding for the other side's problem to more effectively disarm them, deactivating their emotions to bring them back to the man of logic and focusing on finding a solution, among other things.

To achieve this, we are going to cover five different types of techniques. The first is respect and understanding, showing that you understand the other side's point of view to decrease their intensity. Then comes comforting and supporting, letting someone lash out when they are emotional while you persist to try and get across to them.

After that mediation and diplomacy, how to properly mediate a conflict between two other parties without being biased. After that come personal rules and boundaries. This is enforcing a rule and not tolerating something. Sometimes it starts small conflicts, but it also helps prevent bigger ones later in finally focusing on implementation, making a person focus on the solution for a problem and not the problem itself, but using specific wording to force them to do it.

So as you see, we have a myriad of tools that we can use to help resolve this conflict. Let's dive right into them.

CHAPTER 8: RESPECT AND UNDERSTANDING

Let's take a look at the first technique, which is respect and understanding. Here's the thing: you need to put yourself in a lower position than the other person, but you do need to respect them. If the person feels disrespected, that can not only cause a new conflict but escalate an existing one.

Let's take a look at how to average this. If you think of concepts like empathy, connecting, and understanding the other side, they are social skills in general, but they are especially important in de-escalating situations. The core reason for this is that they decrease amygdala activation. You can consider the amygdala, your emotional brain, and it especially activates when you don't trust the other person when you're emotional, such as angry, disliking them, or any other intense negative situation.

Empathy and respect help decrease this amygdala activation, bringing the person back to the domain of logic. But another reason for this is that respect and understanding make people accept something more easily. If you're trying to get the person to make a concession, to settle for something, or just accept something, this will work better if you show that you understand them first, because if they identify with you more, you have more power.

Three techniques work especially well to show respect and understanding for the person. These are, first of all, demonstrating empathy, taking what you think that the other side is fuming or thinking and verbalizing it back to them, saying things like I know you must be stressed or I know you must be frustrated with this, or even I know this is awkward.

This helps calm the person down because they feel understood. The second is to tailor communication for the person's influence archetypes. Four different archetypes correspond to whether the person focuses on the big picture or the details and logic vs. emotion.

For example, if they're focused on the big picture and they're logical, they are dominant. If they're focused on the details and they're logical. They are analysts. Each type has specific language patterns that better persuade them. So, for example, if they're dominant, they don't want to waste time and they want to know how they win.

If you use their language, you can calm them down more easily. Finally actually verbalizing respect for the person. This seems like a very small and specific technique, but it works so well, especially if the person's influence archetype is dominant.

This will be an actual requirement for communicating with them. But in general, especially for people that have an ego or that are sensitive, it's always good to verbalize respect for them, and it doesn't need to be something very sophisticated. Just saying something like, I know your time is valuable, so thank you for being here or I respect your authority and credentials.

You want to understand and respect the person's achievements. One side note you don't need to bring yourself down. You just need to raise them. Specifically, one of the most frequent profiles that you will find is alpha or dominant people.

These comments There are specific techniques to deal with this type of personality, which you will find in any of my books that includes the disk personality types or other resources. But these become important when you have a person that is on edge, and these can include first asking for the person's opinion.

Dominant people hate to be excluded from things, and they love when others ask for their opinion and expertise. So even if you're not going to do anything with their opinion, just ask for it, ask them to validate something, or to say what their thoughts are. This helps disarm them.

The second is showing them how they can win and what they win. It's exquisite. This is all that dominant people care about being better than others. Show them how you can fix the situation and give them something that makes them win. Also, verbalize respect. We just mentioned this.

Show them that you respect their experience, credentials, authority, and status. And finally, you have to make concessions. This is not as much of a technique as it is a necessity. A dominant is your worst negotiation nightmare because they will have everything and give nothing. Whatever you're trying to accomplish, expect them to take a lot more than that and give you nothing in return.

Dominance and specific are. Children who throw tantrums and take their negotiations, if even a little detail of what they want is not respected. You will need to be the adult that takes the hits, gives them what they want, and safeguards the negotiation. One last consideration when showing respect is that dance people can be triggered by a lack of respect, not just for them individually, but for others as well, especially if the party that you're disrespecting is someone close to them, or if they have a heightened sense of justice.

I have to confess that I am this way if I'm in negotiation with you and I see you can align or not hold the door for somebody else that is completely unrelated to us. We're done here and many people are this way. They require you to be decent in general, and it's fun that the biggest example of this happens in the context of job interviews.

The person is on the way to the building, and they could cue or push somebody in the lobby interests and they don't apologize for it. And then later they found out that it was the interviewer or someone related. And they're done. So remember to do things such as waiting in queues without cutting, using manners like please and thank you for holding doors for others, especially near or inside your office building, because you never know who that random person might be to your research before suggesting things showing respect and to be cautious, especially with people that think you are, quote-unquote below you like juniors, assistants, cleaning staff and others.

This happens both with situations in the real world or just in work. If in a crisis, the other person sees you treat a team member like crap. They can be triggered as a client because they assume that if you don't treat your people well within the company, how are you going to treat a client?

Well, which, true or not, is a very fair question. What are some implementation pointers? The first is to treat everyone as equals. One of the best ways to show respect is to show it to everyone, people that you pass by on the street. Service workers, people with different statuses in the company let people see you as respectful under every circumstance.

Be grateful. Being respectful and keeping decorum when others do so as well is easy. Being grateful when you're big attacks, though, not so much. Don't take the bait when others are being less than graceful. Don't just turn it on. Being respectful should be a core tenet in life.

Don't do it just when you're in work mode or with important people. Make sure that it's a personal trait, regardless of the circumstances that you're in. And finally, hold yourself back. Remember inhibiting yourself when others are trying you and beating you into stooping down to their level?

Make sure that you don't, because that's a situation where you will never win. What are some do's and don'ts in terms of respect and understanding do's do, whether we don't think there is no such thing as too much respect? I mean, there is, but it's probably a lot more than what you think it is.

Make sure to act that we show that you're being respectful and considerate so that you don't give the other side a reason to attack you. Don't, don't take it out on people, even people that you may consider that have no status or are below you probably are not. They just appear to be. And even when they are below you, well, you never know where you'll be tomorrow or them.

I know many people that treated a subordinate like crap only to later come work for a company where they were now superior or equal. And guess what happened? Don't give anyone a reason to hold a grudge in the future. What are some examples of showing respect and understanding? The first is just verbalizing. I know this is hard for someone to verbalize to another person that they know how hard the situation is. But then, unfortunately, this change is still necessary and cushions the blow to them.

The second is verbalizing this agreement, saying something like I know you don't agree with this and I know you had your plans, but unfortunately, we will be doing this, for example. It also helps empathize and soften the blow. Finally, another example is paying attention to the way dolphins do go a long way in showing respect for someone holding the door for them, not interrupting them, and so on.

What are our key takeaways here? The first is using empathy. Take what you think the other side is feeling by simply verbalizing it. I know you must be upset. I know that you must think that I'm not being. Reasonable. I know you must think that this is unfair and so on. You don't have to agree with it. You just have to verbalize it. Then understanding showing that you understand them goes a long way.

Don't just force your decision on the first show that you understand their point of view and then say that this is necessary despite it and finally show respect. Many people underestimate the role of respect. You don't need to kiss up, but you do need to make sure that you cover the basics so that the other side is not feeling disrespected.

And remember that you can find all key takeaways on the key takeaways wiki page. Both the Wink and the password are in the book description for convenience so that you can just copy and paste them. So as you see, respect and understanding can be shown with very simple techniques, and they can be used to really de-escalate a conflict and even solve it.

CHAPTER 9: RESPECT AND UNDERSTANDING IN CM

We can easily leverage the techniques mentioned specifically to deal with upset or angry customers. The first is empathy. You want to verbalize what they're thinking or feeling. I understand that you must be angry. I understand that you must feel disappointed.

I understand that you must be feeling betrayed and so on. Remember, you don't have to agree with him. You just have to show that you understand their situation, then tailor language to their emotional archetype.

If they are passionate, inspired by the vision and passion, you want to tell them that you understand how this hurts the vision, the big picture, and their overall mission. If they are dominant, they only care about not wasting time. Anybody wins. So focus on that.

If they are an analyst, they want to focus on data-driven systems, processes, figures, and numbers. So that's what you focus on. And if they are nurturers, they want to feel supported. They want to feel like you hold their hand and that you care about them. And finally, you can verbalize respect.

You can tell them I understand your value and importance. I know your time is valuable and so on. Remember, you don't have to bring yourself down. You just have to raise them.

CHAPTER 10: COMFORTING AND SUPPORTING

Let's talk about comforting and supporting in a whole range of situations from a minimal situation, such as an awkward silence to a very intense one, such as someone being fired. People are going to have emotional reactions and it's up to you to withstand them lashing out until they come back from emotion to logic.

Let's take a look at how this process works. Knowing how to properly support and comfort others is important. There will be two main types of situations where this was needed. The first is comforting someone in terms of minor situations.

This happens very frequently, and often we're talking about whether someone is uncomfortable and you choose the conversation topic that makes them the most comfortable to start a conversation when someone is bothering to keep them company after the here in a place of common or to suggest a change when they're physically uncomfortable, sitting in a weird position.

But then you have the major situations when someone is being humiliated in public when they were told they're not getting that

31

promotion. They have a serious personal or workplace issue or others being able to make them feel safe and supported properly in terms of severe situations.

There is one thing that this has in common with aggressive people, which is that they will have high activation or, in other words, they're very emotional. The only difference is that when people are feeling unsafe or mourning for something, usually they take the avoidance route instead of the aggressive route.

But in fact, they can also take this one as well, which further complicates things for somebody trying to help them. So all techniques that you use should help them lower their amygdala activation here. Some of them are in common with conflict resolution, like showing respect and empathy, which can work. But for these cases, in specific, there are usually two main techniques.

The first is to label their emotions, saying something like I know you must be feeling stressed or I know you must feel safe due to this. But labeling emotions helps the person make them logical and reduces the intensity of the actual emotion. It's a great tactic to use your help to decrease the intensity of that emotion by acknowledging it, and then they become more reasonable. After that, it increases trust in the person.

What I mean by this is when the person trusts you, they feel safer. Therefore, the best person to help someone feel comfortable or safe is the person that they trust the most. And this also means that whatever you can do to increase trust and connection with a person will make your words have more weight, and they will let you design their emotions more easily.

Also important to mention is the fact that in the recovery process, some people can result in, especially if they are close to you, they may lash out at you in specific and blame you in a personal way. This doesn't mean that you did anything wrong. It's just the person displacing their emotional outburst, but it sure feels personal. So when supporting and comforting others, one of the keys is to be able to take the hits to take a few bites and understand that this is not personal.

Just as we discussed in conflict, they are usually going to take one of two stances: hot or cold conflicts. Either they are completely shut down, become cold, avoid reality altogether, or they are going to become too violent, aggressive, or even abusive. And you need to be able to deal with both in more detail.

They can do things such as number one, just avoiding the issue. Running away from it at full speed and not wanting to face it. Or even becoming delusional in not seeing reality. Also, they can simply go cool. They can feel a lot of emotions and have opinions on the issue, but simply do not reveal them.

They switch their emotions off so that they don't feel the pain of the situation. A third option is fake, agreeing. They can pretend to agree with you and just lie to your face to get it out of the way and go back to self-pity. Or they may have some plans, including possible revenge that they're not sharing with you.

And finally, we have good old aggression blaming you, insulting you, shirking responsibility, and shifting it on you, among other possibilities. What are some implementation pointers in terms of comfort and support? First, the focus is to help the person regain function.

The biggest goal when someone is in crisis mode is to help them become functional again. It's not just about removing emotion. It's about removing emotion and creating. The way for them to be able to function again.

Coping mechanisms are key here in crisis management. Also solving the crisis is precisely about making sure that this person has good enough coping mechanisms to help them keep their mental health.

What I mean is that they're all coping mechanisms that may not be enough to deal with this new issue. Of course, it's a sensitive issue to ask how a colleague is going to deal with something but do it. Try and ask what coping mechanisms they do have, whether they are enough, and even suggest some new ones. Gestures may work.

Some people feel supported by conversation and a helping hand. But other people can feel supported by a gift, even if symbolic, either a personal one or by their team or a group of friends. And finally, be fair, if people see you comforting a colleague but not another one when they are in similar situations, they'll know that you're being partial and that is a massive earthquake.

What are some do's and don'ts in terms of comforting and supporting someone? Don't focus on safety. These means don't let the person feel judged or attacked be as open as possible to facilitate their recovery. One sniff of a judgmental attitude and the person can retreat right back to the bottom. Don't rush it.

Nobody has a recovery schedule. Some people can bounce back quickly, but others may take time. Trying to rush someone into recovery in a specific timeline can backfire and make it worse. What are some examples of comforting and supporting?

The first example is absorbing someone's aggression. Maybe you give someone some very bad news, such as them being fired and they take it out on you. Stay objective and whether the hits they're just lashing out until they calm down.

The second example is observing grief. Maybe someone lost someone or something important, and you need to comfort them until they get back up on their feet. And finally, another example is bridging avoidance when someone is withdrawing. You need to keep fighting, assisting, or maybe give them some time and then circle back. Always supporting them until they recover.

What are our key takeaways here? The first is that just like with conflict itself, there are multiple reactions that people may have when they need support. Also, hot and cold are very similar to the types that we've already covered to comfort them, you must persist.

The second is that using, labeling and increasing trust does help. Emotion comes from the amygdala, so any technique that decreases amygdala activation brings people back to the realm of logic. Enabling their emotions and obtaining more trust from them are just two examples.

And finally, expect to take a few hints when you're trying to comfort someone who has very intense emotions. They may lash out at you. It's not personal, it's just collateral damage, and you have to go through this to help them recover. Remember that you can find all key takeaways on the key takeaways wiki page.

Both the link and the password are in the book description for convenience so that you can just copy and paste them. So as you see, there are a couple of techniques that you can use to comfort people and support them, but always be aware that someone that needs help is going to be lashing out until they come back down from emotion to magic, and you have to withstand that process.

CHAPTER 11: COMFORTING AND SUPPORTING IN CM

When a customer needs to be comforted or supported and possibly when in an emotional state, the best thing that you can do is take the hits, let them lash out while you empathize with them, let them so we calm down the existing level of trust that you have with them.

As we saw this coming here, having a long relationship means that they will trust you more so they'll be easier to persuade rather than a customer that you are just now meeting. This also means that if multiple customer service representatives or internal people have had contact with a client, the person that they trust the most is the one that will get them to calm down the fastest.

Using effectively can work here as well, labeling their emotions, saying something like, you seem upset or you seem skeptical or you seem sap will dissolve these emotions and decrease their intensity. But without these elements, do be prepared for them to lash out and keep taking the hits while they slowly calm down and come back to the realm of logic. That's when you can find a solution together.

CHAPTER 12: MEDIATION AND DIPLOMACY

Let's talk about mediation and diplomacy. You would think that when you're mediating a conflict between two other people, it's going to be easier than if you were involved in the conflict. Well, it's not that simple.

You need to be aware that when there is a conflict between two other parties, you have to see the merits in both. And you have to be impartial in terms of who you support. Let's take a look. The capacity to mediate conflicts between other people and remain impartial in the face of them is crucial.

You need to be able to effectively detach the logical facts from the personal opinions of the different parties and then help them come to an equitable resolution for everyone. Mediating a conflict between other people is not that much easier than being involved in one yourself. The same techniques and dynamics from conflicts where you are one of the involved parties also apply here, as do some techniques like internalizing, removing yourself from the personal side of things, as well as discussing from first principles separating the facts from the opinions.

One of the most important topics when mediating conflicts, among others, is to realize which rules were broken. As we saw, a conflict is always a consequence of someone breaking a rule. A person may have offended another person by interrupting them, not listening to them, and stereotyping them in a myriad of possible causes.

It's important to know which rules were broken so that you can both diagnose the cause of the conflict, but also prevent it from occurring again. Restoring trust between both parties and allowing them to work together in the future. You need to ask yourself and ask the conflicting parties as well which attitude may have happened that triggered the conflict?

Was it a disagreement?

Was it someone ignoring the other person, someone patronizing either person?

Was it mutual?

And how serious was it?

And then figure out how to crystallize those rules formally. For example, John feels offended if someone cuts him off while he's speaking, and it's important to do it with both parties. This way, they know exactly what they have to avoid so that they don't accidentally or purposefully trigger the other person and then ask themselves and ask the people involved whether they are willing to work together or be together again afterward.

Is there common ground among them?

Does each side commit to honoring the other side's rules or not at all?

What are some pointers when mediating conflicts?

First, find the trigger. There's usually one key occurrence that triggers that conflict, or maybe the medium one, followed by a serious one that compounded and escalated the original situation. But the point is to find out what triggers each side in specific ways aligned with the company culture. There's one side cause of conflict because they win against an expected company culture, behavior, or on the other hand.

Were they following the expected processes? And it was the other side who took it personally. Make both sides verbalize respect. This is key if people don't respect each other and they are not willing to put effort into solving this, or even if they are, they refuse the state verbally to each other. Maybe none of them should be in the team and finally make the rules clear.

All of us know that some things trigger us, but maybe we don't know exactly what they are. It's important to do the work to dig deep and clarify what specific rules were broken for each side. What are some do's and don'ts when mediating conflicts? Do you know where you can project on people here as well? There may be cases where you're meditating and you're like a person or you believe a person more than the other, and it takes a large amount of effort and willpower to remain objective instead of going with your biases here.

So be aware of this. Don't, don't take it lightly. Conflicts are many times deeply personal. If the person thinks that you're just trying to make this better and hurry up to get it out of the way. Paying lip service to it but not doing anything, they won't be honest and the conflict won't be gone. Unfortunately, this is what H.R. does in many companies in the world.

What are some examples of mediation and diplomacy? The first is a simple argument between people. You're in the middle and they ask you to meditate. Maybe two friends having a tiff, maybe two colleagues arguing over proposals. But this can go very wrong, very quickly.

The best way is to be objective, stating the merits of both people and calling them both down. Then a similar example is a workplace conflict. Two co-workers are butting heads over there. Proposals for something at work verbalized the merit of both in the respect that you have for both and pick the best one.

Objectively, the third and final example is intense aggression. If you're between two people, they just hate each other's guts and things are escalating. You need to empathize with both again being objective and bringing them to the realm of logic, deactivating their emotions. And after that, objectively, from first principles based on facts only.

What are our key takeaways here? The first is to start from the first principles or, in other words, facts and not opinions. Reduce both people's opinions of the core facts and the side of those facts. Only the second is being impartial. You mustn't show any preference for any of the people involved.

Objectively, you state the facts and treat both people with the same level of respect. And finally, look for compliance. Our goal here, after analyzing rules and determining a good outcome, is to know how we can prevent this in the future. And if people aren't willing to work together or to be together after this, there's no point in.

Remember that you can find all key takeaways on the key takeaways wiki page. Both the Wink and the password are in the book description for convenience so that you can just copy and paste them. So as we see, mediation and diplomacy are very important when mediating a conflict between two other parties, you always want to be seen as an objective third party.

You do not want to say anything or make any decision that is going to break that frame because otherwise, your credibility is going to be compromised.

CHAPTER 13: MEDIATION AND DIPLOMACY IN CM

In many cases, you'll have to mediate situations between the customer and your own company, and this can be especially hard when the company is at fault. For example, you know that the product failed and you have to get both people internally to agree to that, as well as convey that to the customer. And on top of that, you'll need to balance both the interests of the company and the clients to do this.

The best way is to consolidate the quote-unquote, trusted advisor. You do this by being honest about both the qualities and the flaws of each side without sugar-coating or making excuses either to the client or internally.

There is a persuasion principle that fits in here very well and is called adversary transparency. This means being honest about things that go against you in that you didn't need a share, but you still do, for example, reviewing a problem with the product or decreasing your revenue by a little bit. Doing these things doesn't decrease your authority.

Scientifically, it increases it. This is the principle that you should use to more easily consolidate the trusted advisor frame. In short, when you have things that go against yourself that you didn't need to say, you still say them. This makes you credible. So don't focus on the opinions or impressions of each side, both internally and the client.

Focus merely on the facts, almost like an investigator gathering data. Focus on those. Be honest about those and use them to guide your answers. And look, you may be between a rock and a hard place. In many cases, there will be no perfect solution that makes both sides happy at all.

In many cases, you can't even make one of the sides happy. What you can do, though, is at least make sure that both sides are as happy as possible or the least unhappy possible.

CHAPTER 14: PERSONAL RULES/ BOUNDARIES

Let's talk about personal rules and boundaries. By this, I mean, when someone breaks one of your own rules, you need to have the courage to say, I'm sorry, but I do not accept this. You would think that this is counterintuitive because it's creating a conflict instead of resolving one. But sometimes you do need to draw the line early on so that people know which behaviors are not acceptable.

And then you have a small conflict early on versus letting it drag on and having a bigger conflict later. Let's take a look. Personal boundaries are key to effective conflict resolution, or more specifically, they help create small conflicts to avoid bigger ones later.

As we know, every conflict derives from a break in somebody's rules. Personal boundaries are how you enforce those rules. It's when someone does something that you just don't tolerate you let them know to their face right then and there.

But politely, for example, if someone asks you to take care of something that might not be your responsibility, you can reply with something such as, Unfortunately, I can't do this right now, or when someone asks you to take notes in a meeting, for example, and that is not your responsibility.

You can apply with I'm sorry, but I'm not in a position to take care of this right now. Or when someone asks you to work on the weekend, you simply say, Unfortunately, I can't. You may have these rules about what you tolerate or not, but enforcing them comes down to personal boundaries, what you accept or not from the people around you.

Although this may seem uncomfortable at first, especially for people that are not used to doing it, very shy, and very permissive because this creates smaller conflicts in the present. They are, however, essential for you to stand up for yourself and not bottle things up; doing the latter will only create a bigger conflict down the road. So by drawing boundaries, you're kind of front-loading the conflict.

You're willing to have a smaller issue now instead of letting it drag on and become very big later in terms of corporate behaviors in specific boundaries is also crucial to stop acceptable behaviors in their tracks from the beginning. Because if you don't draw a boundary the first time or the second time that someone does something incorrectly, they will just keep doing it.

If someone speaks over you or cuts you off at a meeting or you're a woman and they call you honey or act condescending and you tolerate it instead of immediately drawing the boundary. And if this keeps going multiple times, they'll become used to it and just keep doing it. So boundaries are crucial to send the message that the person cannot get away with this, that they can't screw with you because otherwise, they believe that they can do anything without consequence.

At the core of personal boundaries is the mindset that you are not to be screwed with. In short, people have to know that they're not a pushover. You have your limit and people can't cross you. It can be a big limit. You can't have a lot of patience, but people have to know that it will run out if they cross you.

If they try to abuse you, they are going to get a reaction because otherwise you're just a pushover and they can just do whatever they want. Personal boundaries are how you show this. In some cultures, it's known as the concept of showing teeth just like an animal. You have limits that, if crossed, are going to cost a proportionate or even disproportionate reaction. And this inhibits people from abusing you.

The key here is that you don't have to draw boundaries on everything. You just seem very irritating and hard to get along with. But you do need to show this for one or two key areas. People have to know that there is a payment somewhere that they can't cross.

What are some implementation pointers for personal boundaries? The first is to be reasonable. Some people have too many rules and boundaries to the point of being ridiculous. Don't ask me things before 10 a.m. Don't talk about topics that I'm not comfortable with in front of me and many of the rules. Another one is to make it a point to respect other people's boundaries because boundaries are not just for you, but for others.

The best way to have others respect your rules is to respect theirs as well. If you don't want to be bothered during lunchtime and you know a person that doesn't like to be bothered during the afternoon, then you know what you should do for them to respect your rule. Another point is equality. Boundaries are only effective if you draw them with everyone and that?

The beauty of it, it should be an automatic reaction, people must get the impression that this is a part of your personality, that it doesn't change depending on the person. If it does, it loses its effect. And finally, you can draw boundaries on things both big and small. You can draw the boundary on a very big request from your manager to work overtime for multiple weeks or just on people chatting near you at a very high volume when you're trying to concentrate. The mechanism is the same.

What are some do's and don'ts in terms of personal boundaries? Don't select the boundaries that are the most important to you. Don't start fights just to prove a point. Defend what matters to you. Don't, don't be too exaggerated in your response. You don't want to break a relationship or kind of push an ultimatum. You just want to show the person that you don't accept this, but then continue the relationship as is with nothing changed.

It's just that I don't accept this. Everything's fine. What are some examples of personal rules and boundaries? The first is someone refusing to work overtime. Their manager is trying to pressure them into working overtime, and they simply politely reply, I'm sorry, but I can't do it.

This is an example. Another is politely disagreeing with a manager. May give you their actions to follow blindly without questioning and point. We say I disagree with this approach unless you justify it to me. And finally, refusing to be certain names is another one. You may have a colleague that is just acting too familiar, calling you lazy or dumb as a comment.

Even if as a joke, you politely tell them to their face that you will not tolerate this. So what are our key takeaways here? The first is that personal boundaries are how you enforce your rules. You may have a rule of not tolerating a certain behavior, but only by drawing the boundary. Do you prevent someone from doing it?

Boundaries are crucial to stop negative behaviors right away. Don't tolerate overtime or offensive behavior the first time, and the person will never ask a second one. And finally, boundaries can be drawn on multiple topics and for multiple attitudes. Only you know what you tolerate from others.

And remember that you can find all key takeaways on the key takeaways wiki page. Both the Wink and the password are in the book description for convenience so that you can just copy and paste them. So as we see, personal boundaries can be useful both to prevent conflicts that you don't want by removing yourself from them entirely, but also to give people the impression that there are certain things that you just don't tolerate and you create a small conflict now instead of having a bigger one later.

CHAPTER 15: PERSONAL RULES/ BOUNDARIES IN CM

Personal boundaries are best used for personal situations, usually not corporate ones in these cases when dealing with upset customers. It's going to be the case that you are going to be the one observing that others are drawing their boundaries on you.

For example, a customer saying, I don't tolerate this X, Y, Z from your company, raising the price, not having good support, not having a quality product, and so on while handling the situation, though, it may be necessary for you to draw some boundaries on the client.

If they are crossing the line, then we try to blackmail you into getting perks that shouldn't insult you or other unpalatable behaviors. For example, let's say that there was a problem with the product and this problem may have been caused by the client and they call you incompetent or fraudulent.

You can reply with something such as I'm very sorry, but unfortunately, I cannot accept that comment. We are investigating the issue. We'll get to the root cause of it. And this is our responsibility for sure. But unfortunately, I'll have to ask you to not use that language again or similar. It can also be used for unreasonable amounts.

For example, if someone breaks a frivolous product and they want five hundred dollars in compensation, for example, by simply replying, unfortunately, we are not in a position to fulfill this demand. But thank you for your time or similar.

CHAPTER 16: IMPLEMENTATION FOCUS

Let's talk about getting the other person focused on implementation. We are going to use it for this purpose. One of my favorite persuasion techniques, which is implementation intention, is that when you force people to think about the how of something, they are more likely to do it because they're the ones that have to come up with a solution.

For example, instead of saying, would this make you satisfied? Yes or no, asking them, How could we make you satisfied? And they are the ones that are going to have to come up with a solution. It's not a silver bullet. It's not going to make sure that you get your perfect solution, but they are going to focus on one solution.

Let's take a look at how this works in more detail when dealing with conflicts. It's probably basic to say by this point that one should focus on the solution and not on the problem. Sure. Analyze people's rules. Figure out the root cause of why this happened, but it's better to not linger on the problem and to move on to the solution itself.

In practical terms, the best way to make this happen is to use the psychological principle of implementation intention. This is a principle that dictates that focusing on the how of doing something on the implementation convinces people to do it more easily.

This principle was verified at first with a study where they wanted people to vote and to have two groups in one group. They just asked the person whether they would vote for the other one. They asked how they would vote.

Which road will you take? What time of the day are you going? And so on. In short, they focused on the implementation of that idea. And the latter convinced a lot more people to vote. This principle can be applied in any area of life to persuade people more easily.

For example, instead of asking where you vote, how will you vote when selling instead of where you buy? How do you buy the same for coffee? Instead of asking, will you get along with this person asking, How will you get along with this person or how can we make sure this doesn't happen again? And so what?

In most cases, this can be achieved by simply using questions or statements that force the person to visualize the specifics of implementing this change, as we saw. These can include, for example, telling me how we can make this happen. Tell me how you all work together. Tell me how we will avoid this in the future and so on. Or what do I need to do for you to complete this or what needs to happen to get this done?

For example, how can we make sure this never happens again? Or even what would need to happen here for you to consider this a success? Or simply, how can we make sure this doesn't happen? Or tell me what needs to happen so that this doesn't repeat itself or any other question or statement? Remember, you just have to force the person to focus on the implementation of the thing.

The beauty of this technique is that not only will the person come up with a solution, but possibly even think that it was their idea in the first place. This is a brilliant technique, putting it in layman's terms to get someone to collaborate with you when they don't want to. What are some implementation pointers for while implementing puns not intended?

The first is that implementation intention is a principle that can be leveraged for any topic. Just make the person visualize the implementation of anything and they will be more easily persuaded. Also, things are always solvable. Using this technique will make sure that the other side gives you a solution.

Although it may not be the solution that you want, it will always generate a solution. This principle can be used to unblock situations. You can be proactive in asking how to get something done, but you can also use it as a response to a known to unblock options. For example, if someone tells you there is no way that they will be able to work together, you can ask what would need to happen for you to work together. And finally, you can ask about any specifics as long as you ask about the specifics.

What attitude will you need to make this happen?

What timeframe would you have in mind?

What methods will you use?

How can you make it happen?

What needs to happen for you to accomplish this and so on?

What are some do's and don'ts with implementation?

Do make use of this tool in different scenarios. You can always leverage it to get someone to collaborate with you. Don't hypothetically ask this. Use this principle to ask about specifics to get things done. How will you get along with people? How are we going? Preventing this from happening again and so on, is very practical.

What are some examples of having an implementation focus? The first is for closing a deal when you're trying to negotiate with someone and getting nowhere, asking them How can we make this happen? Can make the other side come up with a solution.

Another example is working together when two people don't get along that well, asking the other person, How can you work together? Or What needs to happen for you? Being able to work together can help them think of the specifics that may help the situation. The first and final example is improving something. This technique can be used to overcome difficulties, but also to improve things, asking How can we make this even better may generate interesting solutions.

What are our key takeaways here? The first is implementing intention, as the name says, is all about, well, implementing, forcing a person to think of how to do something which makes them visualize it and come up with a solution? And at the end of the day, more easily do it.

It can be used as a question or a statement. Any format works as long as at the end of the day, you ask about the details of implementing this. Remember, there's always a solution. This technique is very effective because it forces the person to come up with an answer.

It may not be exactly the answer that you want, but they're always an answer. And finally, the magic of this technique is that it'll make the person think that it was their idea if they are the ones generating options. And remember that you can find all key takeaways on the key takeaways wiki page.

Both the Wink and the password are in the book description for convenience so that you can just copy and paste them. So as we see the principle of implementation, the intention is very powerful because you move the person away from the problem and you move them toward the solution.

What you're doing is you're asking questions such as How can we fix this? How can we make this happen? Tell me how this could work for you, and force their mind to focus on that solution. It's very simple but so powerful.

CHAPTER 17: IMPLEMENTATION FOCUS IN CM

Focusing an upset client on implementing a solution is always possible and very simple, it merely consists, as we saw, of using simple statements or questions related to the specifics of achieving something. For example, one specific thing would satisfy you at this stage, or even better, how could you be satisfied with a solution that we gave you?

How could the solution that gives you work for you or what must be done, in your opinion, to resolve this matter? Or tell me how we can address this issue in your opinion? Or, for example, how can the solution that we present work for you or how could you make the solution work, or tell me what specific requirements you have to consider this quote?

CHAPTER 18: TRAPS INTRODUCTION

L et's talk about Traps, here's the thing, even if you're leveraging all of the techniques, that doesn't mean that you may not also be doing the wrong things. So it's important to be aware explicitly of the traps that you can fall into and how to avoid them. There are two major groups of traps, misalignment traps, and escalation traps.

Let's take a look at both. Even if you have properly diagnosed the conflict, you are using the techniques to effectively handle it. There are still some attitudes that you can take subconsciously that can make things worse and take away some of the progress made or even all of it.

In many cases, you may not even realize that you're taking these attitudes and they can have serious consequences for the relationship because they antagonize the other side. We are going to take a look at some of these traps that you can just fall into even when you don't realize it, for you to be aware of them and avoid them during your interaction.

For this, we are going to cover two main families of traps that you can fall into the first or escalation traps. These are attitudes that make the other side angrier or feel disrespected and that make the situation just worse. Then we'll cover misalignment traps.

These are traps that make the other side have different expectations than yours, either on purpose or through negligence by you, and then usually avoid a short-term problem to create a much bigger one later. So as you see in this chapter, we are going to cover the traps that you can fall into then instead of resolving a conflict, are only going to make it worse. Without further ado, let's take a look at them.

CHAPTER 19: MISALIGNMENT TRAPS

Let's talk about misalignment traps, these are traps that result in you not having the same perception as the other person or then fooling themselves in some way. And if you don't fix this, it's going to blow up later. Take a look. There are some cases where you may be the person or marry the person to think something untrue, willingly or not.

And in every single case, this will come back to bite you later because just like any other problem, if it's ignored, it's going to grow and fester. It may be something that you promised that you know, is just not going to come true. Or having agreed to something hastily just to cause a topic that is not exactly what you can do, whatever. But regardless, all of these decisions will come back to haunt you later.

There are three main traps of this type that you should look out for here. The first is misaligned expectations. By this, I mean, you think that one thing will happen, but the person thinks that another thing will. Maybe it's a client that thinks that you're going to get a refund because others in the same situation have and you don't bother to correct them or you're a manager telling a subordinate that this type of work gets them promoted.

And now they're thinking that it will. But you know very well that it's not that simple. The second type is hiring when a situation is too awkward or tense. You simply agree to things that you otherwise wouldn't. Just to get it out of the way, for example, as a manager saying something like, yes, I'm sure you'll get rewarded for the project later.

Just do it now and later. They don't. Or a fruit type, which is you making a false promise? You tell someone to their face that they're going to get something that you know very well that they never will. The problem with all of these is that you're avoiding a current small problem in the present by kicking it down to the future, either to make someone accept something more easily or just to hurry up an issue and avoid attention.

But either way, you are causing a massive problem down the road. And as we saw, any type of problem or letting it grow will only make it worse because the person is going to pile on more and more expectations and assumptions based on what you said as time goes by. So when you wait to have the conflict later, it's going to hit much harder in the rift in terms of alignment.

Will we grow much bigger? The common issue behind this is that many times we say what we don't mean to call attention to. For example, you're sitting with someone important, a client, a manager, a subordinate, and you know what you have to say. But sometimes you just don't dare to say no, especially when the other person has status or authority.

This is, for example, the subordinate that is asked to participate in a project that they know is going to be massive overtime work, and that is going to do nothing for them under normal conditions. They would refuse. But in the heat of the moment, with a boss looking them in the face, they say, sure. And now you are in a prison of your own making. But therefore, the solution is simple as well.

It's to gently persist with your point, regardless of how tense or difficult this situation may be. You need to have that capability to look the person in the eyes, no matter how important, no matter how intense and hold that tension in, not break it. When the other person insists, in short, especially with important people, you will have an immediate reflex of killing the tension when the other person insists, lose that reflex. Don't kill the tension. It's that simple.

What are some implementation pointers in terms of avoiding these misalignment traps? The first is that the more difficult the situation, the more important that this is when someone is trying to extract a big promise from you versus a small one. Or when it's someone of authority versus someone equal. The difficulty level will be much higher, but so is the potential for you to lose a lot more. And therefore the more difficult things are, the more that you think that you can't do it.

The more important it is for you not to give in. Then this comes down to being honest to not misleading others, but also even if you were not the one to do it. If the person is misleading themselves to still intervene and correct them, despite how hard and awkward this conversation may be. This will involve some hard truths.

Being honest and adjusting someone's expectations may make them disappointed or angry. But the alternative is then becoming. Even angrier and more disappointed when this explodes in finally focusing on corrections, on every little detail, even when people agree on the big picture, they may disagree on the details or the timeframe or many other specificities trying to uncover what they think is incorrect when they're not being reasonable.

What are some do's and don'ts in terms of misalignment does make it a point to always check with a person, whether they understand and agree with something. Make this a constant practice so that you never have an unpleasant surprise. Don't think that the other person is fully responsible for what they think because if they have the wrong expectation and you know this and you didn't correct them, you're just as guilty.

What are some examples of traps that cause misalignment? The first is someone getting fired. When the manager is trying to negotiate the terms, they're too nice and they end up promising things that they can't deliver on, such as that they'll pay their full salary or something similar for a couple of months and then they can't. And this type of situation always blows up.

Another one is her antics in a company. What I mean is when someone dies, but we use their manager and open up, we confront them on everything. Casting doubt, imposing on others. If the manager doesn't tell them the truth, which is that they have to go now. But instead lies or sugarcoats it, telling them that they can stay just to kill the tension.

This usually ends up becoming very ugly. Finally, promises made to friends are another example. It may be the case that a friend is falling and you promise them something to go out with them or similar activity when you know full well that you're not going to do it later. And then this becomes even much more of a left out. What are our key takeaways here?

The first is that there are always three main ways to spark misalignment. Having different expectations around the issue or actively promising prospects. Remember, this will always come back to bite your people or take your word seriously, and they'll draw conclusions and assumptions based on it. So you're avoiding a small problem now that is going to become much bigger later on.

Misleading can take many forms active and passive. You can actively lead someone to believe something different from reality or simply not correct them when they do believe it themselves. But it's the same thing at the end of the day, and remember that you can find all key takeaways on the key takeaways wiki page.

Both the Wink and the password are in the book description for convenience so that you can just copy and paste them. So as you see, multiple things can happen in terms of misalignment traps from just lying or not correcting someone's wrong impression when they have it. And if these are not fixed immediately, there's going to be a bigger confrontation later on because those expectations are going to snowball on both sides.

CHAPTER 20: MISALIGNMENT TRAPS IN CM

You can avoid most misalignment traps with an upset client by both not making false promises and by also always correcting them when they have unrealistic expectations themselves. If a client, for example, expects their money back on a faulty product and you can't do it, well, first of all, please don't even mention a refund or anything close to it.

And if they mention it themselves or they think that they can have one, you have to politically correct them in terms of this not being possible, for example, with a personal bond. Unfortunately, I am not in a position to do this for you right now. I'm very sorry. Or if a client expects the company to assume responsibility for something that is their fault.

First of all, don't mention the company having responsibility in the first place, but also when they are the ones to mention it, you have to politely correct them and tell them we're very sorry, but this is not our fault. And I know these are small, awkward moments.

This is true, especially when you have to correct someone that is of high value. But by having these small conflicts now, you avoid much thornier issues later because they disappear now instead of growing and festering.

CHAPTER 21: ESCALATION TRAPS

Let's talk about escalation traps. These are very simple. These are things that you do, such as not showing respect or kind of diminishing the person's problem that just make them angrier and escalate the situation further.

Let's take a look at the main escalation traps and essentially how to avoid them among all the different attitudes that you can take in a tense situation. Some are sure to escalate the situation, and naturally, these should be avoided at all costs.

If you're looking to mediate or to resolve a conflict because honestly, they'll just make things worse, possibly much worse in specific. You should look out for these free, although they're kind of related to each other and can be considered variations of just not caring. They are specific manifestations.

The first is being patronized and or not taking the person seriously, even when you can't do anything to help the person, never make it seem like this is easy, or that it can be solved easily because they don't just make the person feel disrespected and decrees ID and trust. The second one is showing off or acting superior. It's related to the previous one.

This hurts empathy and comes across as disrespectful because the person feels like you're not being honest or you just don't care. And finally, actually not caring or lacking attention, simply not taking care of something or not doing it in time or not doing something.

When you say you are going to do it, arriving late, among other things, this is the opposite of using a personal touch where the person knows that you're putting in a lot more effort than you should hear.

They know that you're putting in less effort than you should, although these patterns are somewhat specific. Your general goal should be to never give the impression that you're too comfortable or that this is too easy because that underestimates the person.

It makes it seem like they're too little or too easy to deal with, or that the problem is not worth your time. And that is a recipe for disaster. When this happens, the person will be angry because in a way they want to see you suffer or not necessarily suffer.

But you want to see you vulnerable, genuine with your shields. No excuses. No B.S. They want to see that you take this conflict seriously. And when you don't, then you don't worry or you're not stressed, the person will just assume that you don't care whether this is true or not. So a technique that works well here is even mirroring their mood when they're stressed. You can seem stressed as well.

When they're worried, you can seem worried as well. If they're angry at your company's department that caused the issue, seem angry at them as well. Even if you aren't just mirroring their mood makes the person assume that you're taking this more seriously. What are some implementation pointers in terms of avoiding escalation traps? First, share the pain.

Mirroring and realizing their feelings helps you show their true understanding of their pain. You're involved in it, and just this goes a long way. Use similar stories. We've all felt similar anger, indignant, or other negative reactions to certain situations. So verbalizing this story where you felt something similar to them helps establish commonalities and empathy. Then be honest.

More than anything, hiding things or not being honest is going to trigger that person and break trust. Don't defend, don't just be honest about what is wrong. Establish common ground, if possible, commonalities help the other side identify with you. In all, empathy and understanding will be accelerated if, besides feeling like them, you are also actually like them.

They will be even easier to persuade. What are some do's and don'ts when avoiding these escalation traps? News does put effort and attention into it because that's showing that you care. Putting in effort is the best technique and its core. The other side just wants to know that you're putting in the effort and honoring the process.

Even if you can't obtain immediate results or a solution, at least show that you're trying to dance. Don't do anything that makes you relate less to the person. Being patronizing, not caring, and being distracted are just examples, but they're not the whole range of attitudes by any means. So in general, avoid anything that will just send a signal.

The person that you don't care about. What are some examples of escalation traps? The first is not giving someone updates, for example, when you're fixing an urgent issue and you promised they give the client some frequent reports.

Maybe every two hours every day and you just don't. Or possibly even worse. You do have an update to send them with good information, but you just don't communicate. This will just make people angry. Another example is false promises.

When you promise to do something but you don't, the person will believe that you think that they're not worth your time anyway, or that they don't deserve your best effort. So be honest about what you can do from the start because otherwise, you're just setting them up for disappointment.

Finally, not matching their mood can also be a serious issue if they are angry or sad. They want you to feel the same way in a sense. If you're happy, inshallah, they will think that you don't care, even if you do. What are our key takeaways here?

The first memory is showing effort, not escalating. The situation in many cases comes down to showing that you're doing everything that you can, showing that you are constantly trying to fix this and that the person has your full attention. The moment that they think they don't have your attention, that's when they start to get angry and escalate the situation.

The second is to let yourself suffer by yourself as Moses out of it. In many cases, when the other side is suffering in terms of something, they want you to suffer as well. So even if you don't have their pain, at least feel their pain. Show them that you are in the final.

We take it seriously, even if you can't do anything more to help the person or you just can't put more time into it. At least have the attitude that you want it to that you would have if you could have that you are at least putting in all the effort to enter the vacation that you can. And remember that you can find all key takeaways on the key takeaways wiki page.

Both the Wink and the password are in the book description for convenience so that you can just copy and paste them. So as you see, there are several escalation traps and you don't want to fall into any of them. You want to make sure that you take this seriously, that other person knows that you're taking them seriously and that you don't disrespect them. Among other elements.

CHAPTER 22: ESCALATION TRAPS IN CM

In terms of avoiding escalating a sensitive situation with an upset customer, always keep in mind to first of all, never make this seem easy, even if a situation can be easily fixed. Stay calm, speak slowly, and say that you'll make all necessary efforts to fix it because they don't know what the necessary efforts are, then constantly communicate.

Again, this is showing effort. Don't make it seem as if you don't have the time for this or that. You have better things to do. Make them think that they have your full attention even if they don't and finally feel their pain. They'll probably be in a state of irritation or anger or distress or others. So don't ever seem happy or even neutral, seem sober, even disappointed, and hurt yourself and sympathy for them.

CHAPTER 23: CONCLUSION

We are now at the end of the Customer Service, Customer Support, And Customer Experience book. We've covered a lot of conflict in this book: how to diagnose conflicts, which techniques to use, and which traps to avoid. Let's think for a moment just to go through all of these chapters and summarize everything with this. We close the conflict resolution.

Our goal here was to learn how to properly de-escalate and resolve tense situations with others to achieve a common goal for this purpose. We covered three main families of topics. The first was the diagnostic being able to properly assess what type of conflict you're dealing with, as well as what may have caused it.

Then the techniques themselves cover the different techniques that you can use to resolve conflicts such as empathy, comforting and supporting, showing respect, personal boundaries, and others. And finally, the traps are the most common traps that you must avoid to productively resolve these conflicts.

What are some questions that you can ask yourself to consolidate the knowledge in this matter? Am I properly empathizing with ensuring respect for others, or am I possibly falling into traps that I'm not even aware of? Do I remain grounded in the facts and first principles while mediating other conflicts in my impartiality? Am I making false promises or at least not correcting others when they have different expectations of me themselves?

Am I both making use of my boundaries and respecting other people? And am I making others focus on implementation or am I dwelling on a problem? Our point of attack for this chapter should be the following. First, make an accurate diagnosis. In short, what type of conflict do you have on your hands and what caused it in the first place?

Then using the tools that we mentioned to resolve the conflict, empathy, respect, implementation, focus, comforting and support, and so on. And finally, always keep in mind the possible traps in avoiding falling into the don't make things seem too easy or disrespect the person or give the impression that you have better things to do, do have the hard conversations to align expectations, and so on.

With this, we close the Customer Service, Customer Support, And Customer Experience. Our goal in this chapter was to effectively solve and de-escalate tense situations. With this, we close the Customer Service, Customer Support, And Customer Experience Book. I hope that this book has helped you with some techniques and some guidelines for conflict resolution. And thank you so much for reading.

ABOUT THE AUTHOR

Sobia Publication

Establish in UAE, Registered in NY and Tokyo. We care about helping others learn to live a better, healthier life. Subscribe for more.

BOOKS BY THIS AUTHOR

Customer Service, Customer Support, And Customer Experience

Customer experience is when you proactively provide great customer care, delight people, and turn them into raving super-fans.

Customer service is when you reactively deal with customer problems, delight them, and turn them into raving super-fans.

Use customer service and customer experience to create happy customers even if at first you have to deal with upset customers and turn them into superfans.

Use customer service and customer experience as marketing and branding strategies because they help you sell more.

Printed in Great Britain
by Amazon

217413db-f426-475b-a6ac-d023144e2bd7R02